I0161332

Secret's

Ernest L. West

Published by Fountain of Life Publisher's House

P. O. Box 922612 Norcross, GA 30010
Phone: 404-936-3989
Please Email Manuscripts to: publish@pariceparker.biz
For all book orders including wholesale email: sales@pariceparker.biz
To request author email: author@pariceparker.biz
www.pariceparker.biz

Fountain of Life Publishing House is committed to excellence in the publishing industry. The Company reflects the philosophy established by the founder, based on Psalm 68:11, *"The Lord gave the word and great was the company of those who published it."*

Book design copyright © 2016 by Ernest L. West. All rights reserved.
Author: Ernest L. West
Cover Design by Parice C. Parker
Interior design by Parice C. Parker
Editor: FOLPH

Published in the United States of America

ISBN: 978-0692733066
05.23.2016

Secret's

Ernest L. West

Secrets

Table of Contents

Ernest L. West

Dedication

I would like to dedicate this book to the person who made me who I am today, by teaching me the ways of God, and showing me through her life how to be a Pillar of Strength. My dear, and beloved mother Ruth C. West, who has gone home to be with the Lord.

Introduction

My thoughts and the foundation of my book Secrets was based on a scenario which happened 6000 years Ago when God created Woman for Adam. However, upon their Creation of unity, they were given instructions to be fruitful and multiply, and let no man separate them. I noticed at the most opportune time when the man was silent, and Lucifer begins to speak. He wanted to separate them.

Speaking through the separation, telling her, she could eat the forbidden fruit was appealing to her eyes. She saw the fruit looked good, and then Lucifer has begun to work on her mind of ambition. He challenges Eve to eat the forbidden fruit, and her eyes would be open. He told her she would be just like God. And she did partake, but quickly realized she had been deceived. The first thing I notice was the power of suggestion. The wicked knew what God had said, but he found out a way to lure her flesh. She thought Lucifer was doing her a favor while at the same time hiding his agenda. Words are a seed, and all he had to do is dangle something that sounds or looked good. He waited to entertain her, and then he took the bite.

This is how I came up with Secrets. This book is a series of events where deception, and manipulation plants it's seed. Often, the Enemy Plant Secret Seeds in our Life, when we are asleep, or not aware of what he is doing. Soon afterward it is manifested, deception will have taken his Root. There are more Secret's you need to know.

Ernest L. West

Undetected

A secret is information of something unknown. The purpose of keeping a secret is to withhold information, in which can destroy. Now, let us go to the bible:

In the Beloved of God, the word tells us of this type of division. He informs us in the scriptures, "Little foxes destroy the vine." It is not the obvious things, but ultimately, your secret (sin) will make you distant, because you have allowed A SECRET (sin), to come in between your relationship. This very thing happened, in the book of Genesis, and the reason God walked through the Garden looking for Adam. Now, he did walk through the Garden every day to meet Adam, but that one day, in particular, it was a different walk. It was a walk of exposing the secret(sin). And he will do the same thing toward you. In closing, do not keep secrets. In the beginning, God gave man and woman one command. He instructed them to stay connected and let nothing separate them. Often, we only look at this command, as an outward act. However, what God was saying, "Do not allow a secret (sin) to come between you." For this is the separation He was talking about, withholding

11

information that will cause distance in a covenant relationship.

It brings discord, but it is the Untreated Small Stain, which goes Undetected. The good news is the way to expose it, treat that stain with a solution, and it will go away. However, here is the Bad News; the longer it is Untreated, the harder it will be to remove. Garden of Eden, The secret (sin) was the very thing that caused Adam to hide from God. As a result, he tried to cover up his shame by using leaves. Think about it. If Adam's secret (sin), caused him shame, and made him hide from God, what would make you do differently in your relationship? If you keep Secrets from your partner, the first sign of division with keeping a secret is shame. Next, the disappointment which will cause you to hiding, and cover up, things from your partner. Now, the covering up act; are the excuses or words that will make it appear as though nothing is wrong. But sadly, the more excuses you render, the harder it will become to explain, and cover up. He will walk through your Garden, looking for you. And in him walking by is the act of The Light exposing your secret (sin) for you cannot hide, and cover up your secrets forever. If you do not come clean, and repent, God will allow your partner, to see your secrets in a dream. For the word of God does declare, darkness was upon the face of the deep. He said, "let there be Light." And The Light appeared out of darkness, causing the darkness to be exposed. The darkness was the unknown, The Secret of the unseen, and when God spoke, The Light uncovered the darkness, or unseen thing person whom you are connected with. Remember, If do you are allowing The Darkness, or the Secret(sin), to divide your relationship? And ,I say again, what God has put together let no man separate.

Invisible Weakness

Fear covered and masked by the egg shell of ego. A lot of men when they were boys have a sensitivity, and if it's not nurtured, then it becomes a feeling of rejection which; has the voice of Fear. This voice is fighting everything on the outside from trying to get in. Notice, over a period, once they become men, there is a particular strong face will appear in the form of a hard shell, that makes people focus on the outside where they will never inquire about their heart! Many men teach themselves that any visible sign of openness, such as crying or showing any passion will show weakness. To prevent anyone from getting inside, they will act hard! Knowing inside that there is a sensitive boy who has never been loved and developed, but hold on! What you didn't receive as a youth, and once you accept Jesus in your life. He will reach back from the beginning, and fulfill you to the end of the serpent's plot.

Don't Smother the Woman

In my belief, marriages have been set up to fail in the world as well as the church. Why? In society, they teach through TV, books, songs, and commercials to be free. If it doesn't work, walk out, and in the church that's not God's word. Let me clarify the difference that will make marriage appear like bondage or slavery! Everyone has a role, and a man should do this and the woman that! They get so caught up in the letter instead of the spirit of Love! Listen! When you talk to someone with pride instead of talking to someone with love trying to make them do something. Let's get real, if they are over 21years old, they don't have to do nothing! They are grown! Sadly, Many men in the church, beat women like a whip with the word. Telling them what the word says! Right there, they lose them! For women can't be smothered or control, and made to do things! She may do it but with some resentment! A woman has to feel free, be given a choice to do things out of liberty! My thoughts! Don't hide behind that shell.

Illusions

In today's world, we have many people who are deceptive. For in their deception, the purpose is to create a certain perception. For example: One angle they may use to curve your view of them is by using manipulation, for they will use their emotions to bring about a certain illusion in regards to their feelings. Ok... let me explain something about this behavior, which can be learned emotion. In ... Hollywood, for the person to get a certain role, they have to get to play a particular character in a particular scene or scenes. To go a little further, they have to become a certain way in their personality to sell the illusion that they have become that person, and this is what make movies great! Actors who know how to sell their roles! Now, the best actors or actresses when you see them off the film, they are the total opposite of their role in the movies. The problem, many people for some reason associate actors or actresses' personality with the role they play the same in the world. However, people who understand characters in a movie know that they are just creating an illusion just for that movie. Beloved this same thought process applies to certain people in the church world, for they will learn how to role-play just to deceive you. And *they understand to get you to relax and to let your guard down is to find a way that you can trust them. And sadly, once you have trusted them, and you have revealed your heart, then they will use your words against you to hurt you. Listen! Those who fall into this category of being a deceiver, Sir or Madam you are exposed. The fact that I am telling this story, you have been caught! And I come to let you know your cover has been lifted. Now hear this! The word of God declares," He will reward every man according to the deeds done in his or her body." Yes! He is talking to you! Now it is time for your reward. Also, the word declares, to them that sow corruption they shall reap the same. Now let me go further as punishment, the reaping is always greater than the sowing! Now Beloved of God let me talk to you for a minute! If you are the recipient of this very act, and the people who have come into your life appearing to be genuine, and an honest friend. Instead, they hurt you, talked about you, and even tried to scandalize your character as a man or woman! Do not worry nor be discouraged! The fact that you did not respond, you did it the bible way. Now watch God on your behalf! For I can hear God say in his word," Vengeance is mine" saith the Lord ...*

Pride Masked in False Humility

Beware of the Snake

One of the signs of pride are when one have done wrong, but tries to cover it up. This individual will make things appear as though, and they have done nothing wrong. For there will give the appearance of being the victim, when they did something vicious. This person will pacify their emotions by gathering many people on their side. And, lastly instead of apologizing they will try to do good well as nice things for you such as giving gifts to avoid having the nerves just to say," I am truly sorry or I apologize. Let me pray for you. Father God touch their heart, and give them peace! Beware of the Snake.

When the Serpent Creeps In

People of God, Beware! There is a spirit of Witchcraft that has unleashed in the church greater than before. Its purpose is to pollute, and Deceive! It is a mocking spirit, and that appears innocent as an Angel of Light! Using scriptures from the word of God trying to Deceive a pull to those babes that are unskilled in the word, and out of the Household of Faith! And in the ending is to impregnate them with the Seed which brings Depression, and Death! This spirit is trying to immolate the ways of God. As the Word says, God will supply all of our needs according to his riches, and Glory! Well, this spirit will present himself as a supply, becoming everything you need. However, here is the catch; It was just a plot for him to get inside of you. Once he is inside of you, everything that appeared Good, will become the total opposite. Just like biting an apple, it looks red, and once you bite, the taste is sweet. Nevertheless, what the enemy hid, was the bitter reaction from the sweet taste, for he injected his poison down inside the apple which will take only a few minutes to destroy after you have bitten into his plan! Beware, and against this demon, I plead the Blood of Jesus and the gates of hell, shall not prevail!

Communication

As humans, we can become so successful in life, but in one area many of us fail to communicate. For some reason, we must feel like the one who is always right in the conversation with someone who we are close to. So that we never listen to them. Another reason is when the person is trying to convey their thoughts, but we don't completely listen, because of the loud sound in our mind of what we want to say. In response when the other person finish speaking, we speak, and our response tells them that you weren't listening! Then, they shut down, and because they did, you shut down too. now, the serpent creeps in!

Listen

The seed of separation saw your parents split as a child, and your feelings are that when things go wrong, just leave. For in your thoughts, inward decision and outward judgment you are divided. And you wonder what is wrong. Listen, Jesus can make you whole. Because if you don't let him heal you, this seed will follow you for the rest of your Life. Lift your hands!

The Witch and the Warlock Disguised in the Church

There are two type of witches and warlocks who are in agreement, in the church. And their plan's are to divide and kill the Elect Seed before they reach maturity. The first witch, purpose is to bring division and to block the chosen from being birthed. And the next, exist outside the church, and his or her purpose is to get inside and plant his seeds of discord. Also, let me explain something else about this type of witch. They are bold in their stance and beliefs. They will let you know that they are witches, on the outside. Strategically, their purpose is to impregnate their bad seeds, into those who are in society, who have an open spirit. These are the people who have suffered rejection, hurt, and abuse. Who feel violated, and unloved by society and by their love ones. Besides, after they have been brainwashed, that spirit will lead these people in the church. And once, in the church, they will cause them to put on an act, by appearing godly and sorry for their sin's. And in their sincerity, openly give their heart to God, through repentance. At that point, they will appear delivered from the snares of the adversary. They will flow in spiritual gifts, by prophesying, and speaking in new tongues. However, they are

22

under cover. Unfortunately, to their misfortune, they avoided displaying, one area of the word concerning true salvation, and deliverance. The scripture declares, in second Chronicles 7:14, God said, if my people which are called by my name would humble themselves and pray, seek my face, and turn from their wicked ways, Then, will I hear from heaven and forgive their sins, and heal their land! That is the word! And I declare to you, and these individuals are not truly washed, in the Blood. For they have a form of godliness; however, they deny the power thereof. They are a wolf in sheep clothing. For some reason, they didn't pay attention to the scriptures, where Jesus stated, we should bear much fruit, and that our fruit remains. Also, to determine who was of his or not. Also, Jesus said, you will know them by their fruit. A good tree cannot bear bad fruit, and a bad tree cannot bear good fruit. Beloved of the MOST HIGH, yes, he has made us fruit inspectors! That is the word! Furthermore, back to you, Dear witch and warlock, did you not know your wicked ways is a fruit? And, your fruit did not come from God, but from your father, Lucifer! Therefore, based on the word, you are exposed! I did not write it. God wrote it! Your father was cast out of heaven, because of pride. Now, it is your turn. For God has declared, he has caused all of you to come from the north, and to assemble the people God. And there,

23

he shall destroy you! O' Babylonian whore! Prepare for your demise! To be continued. Part 2 is coming, where I expose you witch, who was already planted, in the church from the beginning. I will say this; the seasoned people of God know who you are! You have assembled in the pulpit, living a perverse lifestyle. The clock is ticking sir, and madam! You have been planting your tares among God's wheat for way too long. We have notice how you have been leading many souls astray. For this cause, their blood is crying out from the earth, O' Cain. And, I declare to you, Woe!

Judgment!

In the days of old. It was harvest time. So, many from far and near brought the 1st fruit of their earnings and laid it the Apostles' feet. This one couple name Annanias, and Sapphire came to them and lied saying," they gave an offering! What they didn't understand, they weren't just lying to mere Men, but they were lying to the Holy Ghost of God and lost their life. Listen to me clearly, there will be many who will look into the Men and Women of God faces, and tell them a bold face lie! By hiding the truth, As soon as the lie proceed from out of their mouth they will go into Judgment! You better stop lying to the Holy Ghost, or God will judge you! Don't lie to the Holy Ghost.

The Father's Respect

The voice of influence a man is under attack. For within their loins, they carry the Seed of the next generation. Sadly, their power is attacked by the commands that be mutilation. For they are being put in jails, and there their manhood is being emasculated. In the homes, their voice of position weakens, and manhood is emasculated. For what their spouses don't seem to understand is that when you talk to that man around their kids, you are teaching them how to respect their father. It is okay for a Man(their Father) to be talked about or to anyway by his wife or women. This means when the children grow up, and when they are spoken to that way, it is acceptable. Now this is Emasculation, so when you are beating him down, in essence, you are beating down your children, in how they view their father, Emasculation! For they are fought on every side that their God-given touch can't be passed on. Notice, where their seed can receive the necessary balance to lead when they come of full age, because there is something that only a father can give their seed. It's just like an Apple tree, to grow apples you must plant Apple Seeds, and the more the Seed grows, the more the Seed will be like and look like, the seed giver. But, because Father's are not in the homes many of their Seed grow up angry, and confused.

Some young men have so much zeal, but not according to the knowledge they pass the same traits on to their Seed as well! Pray for the Fathers! Do not point your finger!

Mud Slingers

I got to tell it! We have many people today who call themselves a Leader, but they will try to make it their business, to expose other prominent Leaders by saying they are gay. Notice, where there is heat, there is fire but let me talk to those mud slingers. Now, Sir and Madam, the bible says, "we will know a tree by the fruit it bears." So, how is it you can be so straight up, and righteous when your female seed walks like a man, and your man seed got a twitch! Shut your mouth, and be Quiet! Unless what is in your closet will come out! We will see what you are hiding! Simplicity

Side Effect's

People who first come into the knowledge of the truth can easily be captivated by the mysterious or the unknown. This is where the spirit of warlocks who are dressed in a Pharisee robe comes in, and say words that people will need to get a dictionary to understand what they are saying. Where in the world did Jesus use 20 thousand dollar words to teach, but He uses parables. Even the word declares He took the simple things of this world, the things that are not, to confound those things that are considered wise! The gospel is taught through simplicity not mystical magic of big words! So, sadly many new learn the letter of the word, but never hear the spirit's heart of grace and mercy! Keep it simple!

Alter

Today, I would like to look into the meaning of the word side effect. A side effect can mean something we can obtain or perform, and the purpose is a positive result. However, a negative response comes along with it, at the same time. Beloved of God we must understand in everything that is good in life, there will always be a side effect. Even the Apostle Paul stated," when he would do good, evil was always present with him. Therefore, I must conclude that we are in a war between good, and evil, Life and Death. For the scriptures clearly let us know "a carnal mind is enmity against God." That means mutual hate for each other. The Word also states," the spirit lusteth against the flesh and the flesh against the spirit." Therefore, that means we have two opposing things trying to impose its will to be victorious. Listen, People of God, I want to ask you a question, which one will you choose? Now, before you respond, let me share something with you. Good can allow a negative object to come in, that may be destroyed, and through the negative encounter, in the end, become stronger. However, if darkness would allow light to come in, darkness has to disappear because it is exposed. For this reason, over two thousand years ago, Jesus my Lord succumbs to death just to defeat its power, and to take all of its authority. Then come back to life just for us, which snatched us from being lost, and in darkness make us part of us his Light! Again, which force will you choose?

God Has You Covered

Today, I would like to share some insight about those individuals who always find themselves in the same situation. The person who regularly quits jobs never can get along with their associates, or the person who always end up with the same type of man or woman. I would like to start by saying, "in any athletic game, the team that prepares the best, usually wins the game." They accomplish this, by learning the other team's strengths, and weaknesses. Unfortunately, the team that is less prepared, not knowing how to exploit the other team's weaknesses, usually will lose the game. One thing that is important to know, each team will have a certain play or plays they run in the game, which is called their secret weapon. This weapon has a very high success rate of achievement. Making their opponent respond in a certain direction, causing them to become successful! Another fact, you need to know, great teams, and great players always know how to make their opponents react in any direction. This is done, by exposing their weaknesses, in which will cause them to become defeated in their momentum. Now, the weak teams may have some good player's, and some good plays. However, at the end of every game, they will make that one mistake, which will open up a series of mistakes that will cause them to lose most games. However, this same weak team, once they learn how to address or correct those mistakes. Particularly, at the end of the game. Ultimately, they will learn the pattern of winning, and become winners as well.

Beloved of God, I am talking to that association in marriage, and in the Church. To correct our relations in life, and find peace, we must first initiate to examine ourselves. We have to address our patterns and our responses. If every time the end results of our relationship are failing, we have to put yourself in the position of the weak team. In the beginning, the weak team played great, but at the end of the game, because they lost focus, they made one mistake, which opened the door for a series of mistakes to occur. Simply, causing them to succumb to failure or Unhappiness. The bible says we must strengthen those things that remain, which are ready to die. In other words, recognize your weaknesses, your patterns, and modify. If you have a tendency to get angry, when a friend speaks to you a certain way, recognize your weakness. Do not get angry at them, but instead show love. Also, if you always blame your partner, when events are happening unfortunately to you. Recognize it. Instead of blaming him or her, ask God to give you the strength to endure. Sir and madam, if you want to have peace in your church house, your home, and in your mind, modify your style, and you will change the outcome of your endeavor!

One Accord

Today briefly, I would like to share with you a dream I conceived. For in this dream, it will reveal those who have decided to forsake all, and follow Christ. Now, here is the dream. I opened up this gate, and on the inside was this large field. Immediately what I discovered, this field belong to the enemy. Also, I noticed in the middle of this field was a large building, and this building controlled the whole field. Knowing that, I ran toward this building. Once I was able to get inside, I place a bomb there with a timer. Afterward, I ran out the building heading toward the gate. As I was running coming from this building fiery darts, and the weapon was being shot at me, but none could get me. Finally, I made it to gate simultaneously the building and field exploded. Now the meaning of this dream is as follows. The dream represents many Christians who have decided to receive their deliverance. The building inside represents a strong religious hold controlling the mind. Now, when I placed the bomb inside the building represents the word of God. And the fiery darts being thrown were the enemy of our soul turning against us because we had abandon our way of thinking, and decided to make a stand for God. Beloved of God, the reason it feels as though the walls of life are closing in you. And It seems with every step you take there is a fight. It is simply because you have made a stand! Do not worry for the bomb has been activated, and your adversary is about to be destroyed with one sound!

Double Minded

Today if could, I would like to expound on the act of being on one accord. Now some people believe or think only if the person or people do not think the same or say the same thing, they do not agree. I come to say to you sir or madam that is partially incorrect. Now, to speak the same is correct but it is not the whole meaning of being on one accord. For the scriptures go on to say," there are many administrations of gifts." However, the same spirit and it is for the perfecting of the saints.

Therefore, to clarify my point let me give you an example. In the arena of sports on a football team, everyone has a position, and the team that plays together the best will win many games. Listen, on a team, you may have many quarterbacks, but there is only one designated to play in the game at a time. Running back and other positions are the same. Now, the quarterback is not the running back, the running back is not the quarterback, understand this. Each team player who performs their position the best, and is not worried about the other player's position. Learn how to develop a sense trust for each other then that is the true definition of being on one accord, they will compliment each other by maximizing their personal position. Now yes, their assignments are different from each other. However, they are in one accord. Okay, you do not believe me. Let us go to the word. The scriptures declare, "there are nine gifts of the spirit." To clarify unity, the scriptures go on to say," there are many administrations of gifts, but the same spirit." And, it is for the perfecting of the saints that the church may come into the unity of the faith. Now, my question to those who oppose the word of God concerning certain areas of your life, have you received the Holy Ghost since you believed?

Idolatry

Today I would like to talk about the mindset of an individual having a double mind. For to be double minded means to be unwavering, undecided, also having a different mind at different times, unsettled and undetermined. The reason many people in the church, even in the five-fold ministry are not effective in deliverance, healing, souls not being added to the kingdom and not have received the complete blessing of God intended for them to possess is because they are double minded. For this state of mind is a work of the flesh which is at enmity with God. The word of God exposes this type of individual, God states, "a double minded man is unstable in all his ways." The word goes on to say, "let not this man think, he shall receive anything from God." Also, I would like to briefly give an example of his fruit. He will say, one thing today, and say another thing tomorrow. His actions never line up with his word or vice versa. Furthermore, you can ask him a direct question, and his response will be indirect or invasive. He will never feel satisfied or be fulfilled. He is always fancy. He gets bored easy. And, if you remind him of things, he told you he would perform in which he fail to follow through on. He will always have an excuse, of why he didn't follow through with his word. And if he is found untruthful in his actions, there is always a cover up with a lie. He will appear one way through his words, but his actions are the totally opposite. However, sir or madam, I have one thing to say, "REPENT," for such is the kingdom of heaven. You may say God uses you to prophesy! Lay hands on the sick! However, I got news for you. God do not want your gift because he wants your heart first. Now, let me respond to your gift usage; Sir! They are not your gifts anyway, but they are Gods gift. Let me explain; the reason, he gave you a gift is to bring praise to Him. Sir! God wants you to rend your heart, and not your garment. Even though you have a gift, unfortunately, you do not have "the gift." Therefore, on your judgment day, He will tell you, "depart from me you worker of iniquity I never knew you." For, this is "the gift," I am referring to, having "intimacy" with God. For the time has come, I employ you to lose that double mind, and receive the mind of Christ!

Don't Let Past Hurts
Abort Your Destiny

The day we live, I have observed many high profile men under attack. It seems beneath all the accolades, and breathtaking efforts they have been able to perform in their sport. They have many interpersonal issues in their private affairs for years, and many people have focused on these celebrities God has given ability, but never considered the human side. Sadly, once their faults become exposed, their good image turns into hatred. However, the problem began when fans made them their icon or their god. These individuals have been elevated where it was unavoidable that they were going to fall. The bible states, "Pride goes before a fall." Do not think pride only applies to the believer, but also in humanity. All Glory belongs to God. Therefore, when the attention is placed on the gifts, individuals acquire, instead of God, who gave those gifts. He will react by defending His Glory, and pull people down. For, God did say in his word, "He would not share His Glory with no one." He let us know here," He watches over his Glory." Beloved, if you want to see your leader in whatever he or she is leading you to fall. Position him or her in the place where God is only supposed to dwell, and watch God react in his wrath. However, if you want your head to always have God's favor; by no means make them your idol! Don't let the memory of your past hurt keep you bound

Pride

Are you in a mental fight with your memory. Today, I would like to encourage you In your own warfare. Every time a good thing happens to you, bad thoughts are there to pull it down. Be encourage, I know you feel trapped, and I know you don't want to feel the way you do. Let me tell you what is taking place. You are ensnared. You are caught up in the trade winds of your times. But, I come to bring good news from the throne of God. For, there has been a small cry in your heart for help. For that reason, I have come to declare unto you that God has heard your petition! For, I can hear the word of God declaring, "The Righteous cry and God hear their cry, and He shall deliver them out of all their trouble. For, God is saying, "I am come down to help." Beloved, in a moment and the twinkling of an eye. There is coming a rapture. Jesus is going to crack your spiritual skies of oppression. He is going to snatch you from your bad memories. God is going to bring you to a place, where you have never been before. He is going to make your captivity captive! Where you will have authority over everything that is in your mind. Now, I speak to you! O'Spirit of bitterness, and rejection! Loose, your hold! i take Apostolic Authority over you! LOOSE THAT MAN AND LET HIM GO! For the word of God cancels your word. The Axe Head of the Gospel is laid at your root. Now, come up and out! COME FORTH LIBERTY OF GOD! Arise! And, guard the walls of their mind with your sword drawn, and execute any residue that would try to enter in again! Now, God, we thank you for deliverance. We are grateful to you for your power. We thank you for setting your people free! And we will not be entangled in bondage again in Jesus name! Amen.

Unforgiveness

Today we are living in a day where many people are full of pride. Particularly, against receiving correction, from the word of God. For, they are so full of themselves that they believe their opinions are equivalent to the Word of God. Amazingly in their intellect, they build up strongholds where they attempt to strive with God in their observation. For when people make an attempt to correct their view, according to the bible, they become insulted that a person would have the nerve to defy their thinking method.

Let me explain, the reason of their strong thinking position, they have become so content in how they think. In this comfort zone, they have built a guard around their opinions, where they have become relaxed to the point that they do not want to change their views. For, they only will pay attention to their intelligence. And If any voice would try to penetrate their belief, to them it is considered an intrusion. In that viewed intrusion, the person who challenged their views, they will begin to mock, twist, and belittle their words for a laugh. Not knowing the words they use were not their personal words but the Word of the Lord. For, they thought they were smart with a man or woman, but actually, they were mocking God's Word. And as a result, their mind become a god! However, I declare unto you Mister Pride! The word of God states, "be not deceived God is not mocked, whatsoever a sows that will he also reap." Dear sir! You are trying to get a rise out of that person to do sport and mock them, but out of your own mouth, it will be your own downfall! Just as the walls of Jericho fell, the walls of your intellect, which is your comfort zone, are coming down! Did you not realize Jericho! That God has sent spies to Rahab who lives on the top of your wall? And she has given God's spies access to your kingdom which will make you become powerless O' Jericho! Also, considering that you have been practicing iniquity in your city everything inside I will destroy O' Jericho!

Lay Aside Every Weight

Today I would like to talk about forgiveness. Forgiveness means to refrain from imposing punishment on an offender or demanding satisfaction for an offense. Also, to forgive is having a change of heart about a person. Also, it is to extend mercy to someone and to remember the act no more. Now, there is UN-forgiveness. UN-forgiveness says an eye for an eye and a tooth for a tooth. Meaning whatever you do to me, I am going to do it back to you. In fact, I am going to make you suffer badly. Every time I think about what you have done to me, and I will punish you severely. I will not kill you, but I will always be in your mind tormenting you until you surrender. Beloved, what people do not realize is an unforgiving heart is a wage of sin. And the bible states, the wages of sin is death.

Beloved, do not become trapped in the prison walls of having an unforgiving heart. The results of an Unforgiving heart bring sickness, disease, and ultimately death. It is like having small cancer, if not treated it will spread through the whole body. Jesus has the key that will unlock that gate. And that key is love. The word declares God so Loved the world that he gave his only begotten

Son that whosoever would believe in him would not perish, but they shall have every lasting life! (John3:16) Also, the word declares, your yoke is destroyed because of the anointing!

Be Steadfast

Today I would like to talk about the scripture, which states that we should lay aside the weight, and sin that so easily beset us. Weight means the force that gravitation exerts upon a body, equal to the mass of the body times. The effect of weight: it can cause strain or weakness carried over a period.

In our everyday journey. We all work hard to find rest at the end of the day. Every person's dream in life is to find a job that we can work less, and make a lot of money. Sadly, you will notice the people who work the hardest will not make equal value when it is time for them to be paid. These workers will never take a vacation because of their budget. However, there come a time in a person's life where they get tired of working hard, and struggling to make ends meat. They become fed up with not having nothing tangible, at the end of the day. First, they rebuke poverty and every generational curse that has plagued their family. Then, they noticed in their family line, and their grandparent was always poor. And, many tell themselves it will not happen to me. The next step, they ignore the fear of failure. Then, they change the type of friends, who are full of doubt and always negative, to friends who talk faith, and positive.

And because of their changes, their concepts changed, in which caused their surrounding of friends to changed. Now, their outlook on life has become different. Instead, of looking at life as being a victim. Now, they look at themselves as the victor, someone who can accomplish his or her goals. It only took making a decision, where they did not accept anything negative rebuking their past. Changing their friends, and now the weight of failure has lifted. Beloved, if you notice, the people who doubt themselves will fail. But the people who become successful are always positive.

There is a spiritual principle at work here if you want to stay defeated embrace doubt. However, if you want to have a victorious life, have faith in yourself, as well as in God. In my conclusion, for us to have everything God intends for us to have. We must lay aside every weight, and sin that does so easily beset us. The weight is our mind, and our sin is our imagination. Do not let your thoughts or your imagination keep you from the blessings God has intended for you to have on earth. So many people are living beneath their privilege because they embraced someone else's fear's, and doubts.

Be the person who God intended for you to be, that is, His son's and daughters of the cross!

Wisdom

Once upon a time, there was a woman who feared God. She was a person of great monetary possessions. She acquired her assets in the course of tough, physical labor. But there came a time, where the more intimate she became with God, her natural possessions were taken away.

For, there was nothing she could do in her own strength to save her possessions, because if she would have tried to save her possessions, she would have lost her devotion to God. Therefore, the time had come, where her devotion had to mature in God. For, she would need to stay strong for the reason that at the end of the test she would receive double for everything, she had lost. So, for her to receive her compensation, she had to endure some heavy adversity.

Listen! All through the moments of her wrestle with her tough trials of faith, there was an influence telling her, the faith she was professing was only an excuse not do nothing, by not responding to her warfare through deed. But, she still stayed unwavering in her faith, despite the fact that the influence even tried to assassinate her character, as a woman.

But finally! One day, what God had promised her, happened. And all God had promised her was rewarded. First, she gave God the praise. Then, she gave God thanks for giving her the strength to endure. Now the negative voice that was plaguing her stopped talking! Beloved of God, the Word of God declares, "be ye steadfast unmovable always abounding in the works of the Lord, for as much as you know, that your labor is not in vain in the Lord!"

Unpopular

For those who are starting out in a relationship or marriage! Never invite your friends into your union for counseling, because of their personal attachment toward you, because they will become partial two you, instead of the welfare of your union. For in emotions, there are many mistakes, and it's not a matter of who's fault, but just a bad choice of judgment plus the lack of wisdom! If you need help, always find a certified objective counselor, who doesn't have an emotional attachment to neither party! Wisdom!

Substance & Character

Today I would converse about the position of unpopularity. By definition unpopularity is the total opposite of popular. One definition is to be unknown, disliked or not received. For the reason of something is not received can be based on its appearance, something that appears dull or unwelcome. Now, in the word of God, there was a prophet named Elijah. He was unknown by the general public. For his purpose was awaken, when sin had become prevalent, and there was no repentance in the land. At this place, out of nowhere, He appeared speaking to the king, declaring unto him, because of the sins in his land, rain will not come down for two and a half years. He also stated, "accordingly to his word." This thing would not happen. Now, look at this, here comes a Man unknown to the public, but because of sin, he Shut up the heavens. And as a result, of bringing bad news to the king, He became unpopular and disliked by the authority figure in the land. For the prophet knew the king had the power to take life, just by speaking a word, for this reason, after he delivered his message. He ran for his life and hid under a juniper tree. However, What I love about God, when you stand in your position, as a believer against unrighteousness. The impact of exposing sin may cause you to hide *under a juniper tree. But while you are under your juniper tree experience, God will send an angel to touch you. Not only will he send you an angel, But he will send a Raven, the most unpopular bird in the world to sustain you. A bird typified of those people that are considered dead, unwanted, and selfish. God will cause them to supply your natural needs. For, the word the Lord does declare, "when a man ways please God, He will make his enemies at peace with him." So, if you are sensitive to God's voice. And because you have obeyed his voice, but you find yourself all alone. Do not allow your loneliness to effect your vocation in God. For the word of God states, "Woe unto you when all men shall speak well of you." For so did their fathers to the false prophets. Know this! If men hated Jesus without a cause, as his seed, they are going to hate you! Because to be a friend of the world, is to be an enemy of God. For the word of the Lord says, fear not, nor be dismayed, at their faces, for I will protect you and sustain you. Be encouraged! You may feel unpopular with the administration or principality in this world system. However, I declare unto you, obey God's command. For, your unpopularity on earth, is popularity in the kingdom of God. Therefore, speak to Ahab! Tell him because of his sins. His kingdom shall be destroyed!*

Underestimated

Often people get so caught up with things, such as nice cars, jewelry, money, a beautiful woman, and an attractive man. Notice, these things easily deceived people but never take the time to look for the things that which come from within. Often, the person who are flashy only flashes because they know someone will respond. For on many occasions, the people who act like they got the goods are truly the one's who don't have, but they have learned the game was to create the illusion of substance. But the true people who possessed the good don't have to flash. These individuals can drive a beat-down broken car, but what's inside of them when they are seen will you think that they have a Rose Royce! The car doesn't make a man, and the man makes the car. For the true substance that one possess it's not just in their words, but become the very essence of who they are! Substance and Character!

Blind Spots

I would like to talk today about the word underestimate, which is defined as to misjudge or to estimate inaccurately. Once upon a time, there was this young red lad, named David. He was the youngest of his seven siblings. Every day, when it was dinnertime, he never ate with his brother's. He would only receive the food that remained when everyone was done eating. At times they would have a feast; the boy never invited, because he had to take care of the sheep. Even, during wartime, he wanted to help fight with his brothers, but because of his age, he was only allowed to bring his brother's something to drink. David was never included in anything they would do together as a family.

However, there came a time where God was seeking for someone with a perfect heart that He could trust. God sent a priest down to a man's house name Jesse, to anoint one of his son's to become king. Immediately, he made his son's stand before the priest, but not his youngest boy. First, the priest went to the eldest son. He looked strong outwardly. He spoke very eloquently. Surely the Lord would make him king. But, the Lord said to the priest no then Word of God came *saying", man looks at the outer appearance, but God looks at the heart." Then the priest went to the next son and the next but none of them God chose. After that, the priest asked the father, do you have any more sons? And he replied, yes! But he is a boy, who takes care of the sheep. And the priest replied, bring him to me. We will not sit down until he arrives. Once little David had arrived standing before the priest, God said, "he is the one I have been searching for!" Now, this entire boy's life, he was never included when the family would do things together. His handicap was his size and his age. Sadly, what his father did not realize everything he did not give his son. His Heavenly Father would give it, through his time alone with him, when he was attending the sheep. And every negative thing his father ever tried to bestow upon him or deny him, where the things that made him strong. The bible states, "the stone that the builder has rejected has become the head cornerstone."*

Beloved, you may not converse the best, nor you may not be the most popular among your peers. You may have put your trust in certain people, and you were always there for them, but when you needed them the most, they were never around. On many occasions, they may have known what you were dealing with, where God spoke to them with the answer to your problem. But they would refuse to give it because of their personal issue with themselves. Do not worry, because what they omitted to give you as a friend, or confidant. God will cause your answer to be birthed through their disobedience. The doors they closed on you, God will open greater doors for you to walk through. Beloved, in the end, they may have viewed you as a boy, but God views you as a man. They may have viewed you as appearing weak, but God views you as being strong. They may view you as not qualified, but God views you as His choice. Be encouraged because everything man thought about you, God thinks the total opposite. And all those negative people who tried stop you from reaching your destiny because they underestimated you, and their hate caused God to make you great in His kingdom!

Address the Source

We all have Blind-spots. There are some things about ourselves that we just can't see. This is where someone who is close to us becomes valuable because they can see our Blind-spots, and a true friend will risk losing their friendship because of Love that has for them! Now, that's the core of a true Friend. Not just one you always laugh with, but sometimes you have to get in the trenches, and get serious!

The Cracked Window

Once upon a time, there was this guy. Who had a woman who loved him dearly, but he decided that he needed to hang out more with all of the fellas. He wanted to find out what is was he was missing, and believing his woman would always be home waiting. Finally, what he thought he was looking for from the fellas wasn't there, discovering what he was missing at home. Sadly, once he got home, she was already gone! Listen, the grass will always look greener on the side, but once you get close enough, you will understand, what was missing wasn't in a person but in an act where he felt rejected as a child, due to his father leaving his mom. Therefore, he tried to supplement the rejection he endured as a child by surrounded himself with many people. Instead of facing his woman, to receive healing! Listen, we cannot look through a window clearly, when it has a thousand cracks! The window has to be replaced, to see and it starts from within!

REPENT!

Under Pressure

When you were born, it was a Miracle, when you conceived a child, it was a Miracle, throughout your whole life, you only receive tremors, from an earthquake. And the reason that you received only tremors instead of receiving the full impact was your way of knowing who was in control of your life, but instead of giving thanks? You turned your back on God, and walked away from his hedge, then went to worship other godly Idols. Listen, many things God protected you from, but your pride wouldn't let you see it. Notice, when you removed your hedge, you just opened yourself up, to feel the full brunt of what you were protected! Prepare for things in your life to become touched. You thought that your life has been hard, now the scripture has been activated in your life. The way of a transgressor is hard, and the wages of sin is death, things will begin to happen that you can't control unless you turn your heart back to God and Repent!

It's not too late, turn!

Arise Under Pressure

At an early age, you will learn how to respond under pressure. At the football game, when the chips were down, u responded under pressure. In the basketball game, your team needed a shot, and you responded. In your mind when all eyes were on you something inside of you would Come Alive and Soar. Now, you are in the Real World of life, and something has hit you hard in the chest. This blow has taken your wind, and can't think straight. You can't read your bible right, you can't stand still enough to pray, but all you do is meditate on God's goodness. Now, in your meditation, God has re-kindled a small fire inside. Day by day that fire is growing, but still life is beating you upside your head. You feel like quitting, and walking away from everything that you have believed in. All of a sudden, your fire has become a flame! All eyes are on you, the clock is ticking, souls need to be saved, demon's need to be rebuked, and then u arise under-pressure!

Weather through the bad

Rhythm

Do you want to know why you have not reaped your full blessings? Let me tell you why. Do you remember those Bad Seeds? When you have done those Bad acts? Yes! God did forgive you, but you still have to reap! Listen, God won't break one promise to fulfill another. Yes! He will be with you, through your storm, but He wont' remove it. In His word He says," my grace is sufficient and His strength is made perfect in your weakness. So, you must weather your own harvest! Let me explain: to get to the mountain top harvest, you must endure your valley harvest, and once you have reaped the Bad, then you will receive your good harvest!

I Come

There is a string from me to you, and the more I pull, I come. Sometimes, it feels as though, that I am under some rocks, but I keep holding on, and I come. For there are moments, that I get lost in the sea but at the bottom of much water, I come. Can you feel the rope pull? Yes, I am holding on, ssssh Listen, I come. Now, I can sense that I'm getting closer because I can feel your temperature dose, I come and, then we touch! The Essence of much, awaited space is over four at this moment but I am here! Now stand, then can you come, closer to me and see that our rhythm has become one.

Be Accountable

On the sixth day after God had created man. He gave him dominion and authority over the earth. However, as time transpired, he became lonely and unfulfilled. God seeing his loneliness caused a depth to come upon him. From his side God brought forth bone of his bone and flesh of his flesh, he called her woman. Therefore, the Word of God instructs this union. What he has put together let no man separate! Beloved of God, Today, we live in a day, where marriages are under assault. The thing, God, instructed us not to allow in our marriage, is the very thing that is happening. However, I declare to you, do not kill your connection. Because the person God has connected you with through marriage, in which you are killing with your hateful words, could be the person you need to help you reach your destiny in God. The problem, people, have this theory on who is always right. And sadly, neither person will nudge on their viewpoint. However, I got news for you. Equally, God holds both of you accountable. Together you must find a way to agree. Someone has to abandon their viewpoint by humbling himself or herself, and hear what God has said about unity. Come together, and reason together! You need to do whatever it takes, accordingly to the scriptures to stay connected. For we know the

thief comes to kill, steal, and destroy. However,
God comes that we may have life and that life
more abundantly. Abundant life birthed in
relations is to find a way to understand the other
person's emotion. And once that understanding
received, the mystery of being connected comes
revealed. This is how marriage, obtains the favor
of the Lord, and their held up blessings are
released!

Get the Enemy Out of Your House

Perpetrating a fraud: in the world the divorce rate is between 40 to 50 percent, but in the church it's about 79 percent, and you wonder why? One, probably I find in relationships in the beginning people are fake. How may you do say people are like hypocrites. What do you mean? Example: in the movies when Denzel plays a character, he must become that role to deceive his viewers, just to have best selling movie! You see, the reason why most marriages fail is that at the foundation of their relationship toward the other person they are selling a role to win. Sadly, down the road a piece once they show them their true face, then the other person will say, "they have changed!" No, you never knew them, why? Simply, because they were a hypocrite!

You Will Reap What You Sow

No man can enter into a strong man's house, and spoil his goods, except he will first bind the strong man; and then he will spoil his house.(Mk3:27) This has happened to you in the spirit of your mind because you entertained other things, which appeared right, and good. You allowed the enemy into the house of mind, and now every time something happens to you in your life, you automatically assume the worst. Your mind had become full of doubt, and disbelief instead of having faith like you use to before you invited other things besides God into your house! Turn back to God. and run the enemy out of your house!

No Shortcuts

AUTHORITY: One of the things that you must understand, when the word says, "whatsoever a man soweth that will he also reap!" It's the truth. People who never submitted to authority always acted unruly, and defiant! Life does have a sense of humor! How? You may ask. One day life will flip it where the same person who didn't listen, will be put in a position of authority where they want people to listen to them, but what happens just like they turned a deaf ear, others will turn a deaf ear to them! One way or another, you will Reap what you have sown, there are no shortcuts around it!

The Bastard Child

It's timeout for people who say that are a Child of God, who never read His word nor live in the House of his Presence, how can you be Fathered, if you never come home? Now, you may be a Child of Him, but you may be considered a Bastard Child! Living on the outside, but that's okay. Did you know, based upon the Law, David was a Bastard Child, but because of God's mercy, he was invited in? This is why He said in Psalms, "I was glad when they said unto me, let us go into the house of God!" Come on in...(Deuteronomy 23:2)

Spoiled Goods

One of the biggest reason's why there are so many break-ups today because people just don't listen, misunderstandings take place because of this, some of the problems, friends giving bad advice, one is to follow your heart! One thing about the heart, it can be deceived, especially when an attraction is based solely on a feeling. What's sad, people hear what that want to hear. For when a man or woman tell you, we can just be friends and people who are on a mission will say in their heart, I can make them change. It's all said and done, their feelings have been hurt and will accuse that person of misleading them. It was really their problem of not listening, which caused them to bring it on themselves! Love is a choice and not manipulation tactic!

Submit to Authority

The enemy cannot come into a man's house unless he first Bind the Strong man, and spoil his goods! Many people today who once were strong in their position has now become spoiled! Why? Because they lowered their godly standards, as a result, the enemy came into their house, causing everything about them to become spoiled! The way they walk, talk and think has spoiled their goods! So that, it has caused them to become exiled inside their very home! you can't submit to authority

A Title

To get married, you will need a license, buying a house or car. A title is needed to prove ownership. Notice when a person wants to drive, they must obtain a drivers license. Besides, to be recognized in a position, there will be a proper binding seal from your state authorities that says, "It is so." But why in Church many people fight against leader's having a title when it is written in God's word! The root many people fight it, because they have a problem with submitting to Authority! Point blank man's control.

The Fruit Bearer

One of the things I have noticed from some of our leaders in the church today is they have said, "God is not the author of confusion." Also, they will declare, God does things decently and in order." However, there are times when they will take the scriptures out of context, and spin it for their own interpretation. Not really regarding the scripture in the book Peter, which declares, "the word of God is not of no man's private interpretation." Many times God Spirit will flow from an anointed vessel with the word of wisdom, knowledge, or prophecy. For God has given these vessels to the preacher to develop them. However, because of their lack of knowledge in the word, and sensitivity in the spirit. These leaders will try to become God by controlling His direction for them in their life. Unfortunately, failing to apply the scripture which declares, "Quenched not the Holy Spirit," not understanding the movements of Gods Spirit. Also, not understanding Gods order did not mean to control His order by fleshly understanding, but His order comes from a spiritual understanding. The problem these leaders try to equate people minds to men's logic. For the scripture says, "the natural mind cannot perceive the things of God." It cannot be perceived because it is not spiritually correct. Sadly, they will become a hindrance to Gods purpose by not knowing they are the necessary ingredient that will bring forth Gods purpose in many, just Listen! These leaders are blind for their purpose. You see these leaders because of pride and the desire to be praised by men. Noticing, they will make it appear that they are always right in every word. However, I declared unto you sir or madam. The word says, "There is a way that seems right unto a man, but the end of that way is destruction." For the Word also declares, "the ax head is laid at the root." Now in the word of God, there was the parable of a man's field where he grew fig trees. In this, field all of the trees yielded its fruit, but one. Question? How can a tree become barren in a field that is fertile? Selah! Now back to this man's field. One day, this man came to this field to pick from a fig tree, but he found it barren. Immediately he instructed that the tree be cut down because it had not bared fruit. However, the owner dresser of the vineyard asked his Lord, to give him one more year, and if doesn't bare, it could be cut it down. Beloved, this message is to those leaders who are not being lead by Gods Spirit, but the spirit of their flesh. Leader, God, has made you a Stewart over His possessions. God has given you the necessary tools to bear fruit, and for your seed to grow. You will need to give it the proper ingredient that it may flourish which is Love, not selfishness!

77

Therefore Sir or madam my question to you? Are you holding back what God has put in your spirit to release to them? If you are holding back this scripture is for you, for the word talks against selfishness declaring, "he that withholds corn, the people shall curse him, but blessings shall be upon the head of him that sells it." Listen! Be not intimidated by the people God has given you. Now it may appear that they can preach, prophesy or even pray better than you. But, you must realize, and they are just an extension of you. The greatest pleasure for a parent is for their child to go farther than them in life. Rebuke jealousy, envy, and strife. For the word speaks against such declaring, "jealousy is as cruelty to the grave." Allow God to use you that your seeds may blossom. For the word does declare, "he that is planted in the house of God shall flourish in his courts." Do not try to control your seed's, but guide them in the way God wants them to go, and not in your way. Teach them to be obedient, and you will be rewarded when God comes back to your vineyard to inspect your fruit.

Pray for the Father!

Crippled by Guilt

Many people in society today are walking under some type of control or another. Now, when a person get put in jail, they have to abide by the rules and regulation of that system. For they are told when to sleep, to wake up, to eat and play. This same type of authority controls many with guilt! In many, the origin of guilt started as a child, where they were Emotionally abused, or they hurt someone so bad that they vowed never to hurt another soul, which was sheared in their Emotions! So, because they were deprived of a certain type of attention that they didn't get or again. Beforehand they had a Bad Encounter where they hurt someone! And by carrying this all of their life, when a person tries to play on their emotions, they can easily become persuaded! I curse this seed! Jesus took all the shame, the guilt every sin that we had committed was nailed to the cross! Therefore, we are not bound by Guilt! Double Trouble.

Double Trouble

You have been talked about, and held back. You have been mentally, emotionally beating down and abused. But your adversary didn't know what they were doing. For with every blow that you was hit with, it was only adding fuel, and to increase the Anointing in you! So, what you were yesterday cannot touch who you have become today! You may can't see it, but I can feel your ground shaking! You have took every blow, and you are still standing! And with this last blow, the volcano down on the inside of you is about to corrupt! Prepare for your Holy Ghost volcano explosion that is going to take place now!

Attachments

There was this woman in the Bible, she wanted the promise so bad, that she disguised herself to get it. Yes, She did! She only could see it, but couldn't partake, for she was excluded from this promise! This message is to the pimp and the great madam in the pulpit! I'm not scared to say it, and I'm not scared of you. Yes! You do have the big church and the money, but how did you get it? Did you sleep between the sheets to sleep your away to the top? Did you lie, deceive or manipulate others to get it? Listen, I got bad news for you. You did get the money! But in this next move of God because you sold your birthright for some money! You will only see God's move, but you will be excluded from partaking thereof! Yes! I said it! Now, get off of me!

Do Not Kill Your Connection

In today's world, I understand that it is critical to be connected to someone. For in connection, there is the power of agreement. To back this up in the word of god ... he states, "where there is two or three to agree upon anything that they ask in my name, it shall be done." Okay, now that we can support agreement from what God said! Now I would like to talk about another type of agreement. The first was positive which comes out of the agreement, but I want to talk about negative attachments, which is an agreement as well. What is a negative attachment? Let me give a few examples ... When you get a pain in your chest, the voice that speaks from the pain says, "you are having a heart attack." Also, when there are sharp pains pounding your temporal, that voice says," you are having an aneurysm." If you have a home but you have just lost, your job that voice says," you will be homeless and die from starvation. Beloved of God Just like Hezekiah had done when he got a letter of doom from his enemy. My question to you, what did he do? Let me tell you, and he spread that letter before the Lord. As a result, God moved on his behalf. So what! You have chest pains, and it does not mean it is a heart attack! So what! You have sharp pains pounding your temporal. It does mean it is an aneurysm! So what! You have lost your job. It does not mean you will not lose your home, and die! For I can hear God declaring in His gospel, which means good news, you will not lose anything for the sake of the gospel, but you shall receive one hundred fold with persecution in this day, and time! In closing, let me give you a Rhema Word from the full council of the mind of God which declares, "I am come to deliver you from your negative attachment that brings a negative voice! Saith God!

Acknowledgments:

I would like to acknowledge many people in my life who have instructed in me being the person I am today. First, I would like to Thank My Lord, and Savior for extending Mercy, and Grace to me. Lord, you have Shaped me in the reflection of your Likeness. I would like to Thank my Spiritual Father Doctor Melvin Mosley for teaching me the way of a Man, and Man of God. I would like to Thank All of my kids Ernest Benton (West) Jazmin, Dominique, Daniel and Dylan for being so Special to me. My Beautiful Wife Crystal West for Sticking with me through the dark times in my Life, for being herself and so supportive.

Prophet Ernest West

Contact Prophet Ernest West

www.ernestwest.org

Fountain of Life Publishers House

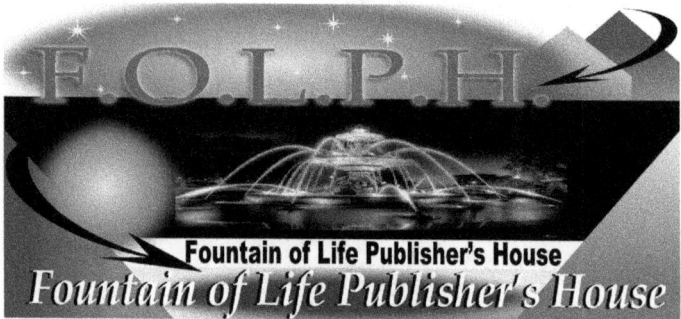

P. O. Box 922612, Norcross, GA 30010
Phone: 404.936.3989

For book orders or wholesale distribution
Website: www.pariceparker.biz

www.ingramcontent.com/pod-product-compliance
Lightning Source LLC
Chambersburg PA
CBHW060554100426
42742CB00013B/2556